Illustrated by ammardegas.

Published by White Feather Press. (www.whitefeatherpress.com)

ISBN 978-1-61808-190-2

Printed in the United States of America

# White Feather Press

Reaffirming Faith in God, Family and Country

# From the Author

Whether you are a firearms owner or not, all parents have a responsibility to educate their children and prepare them for the world we live in. Firearms are a part of our world. In the United States, over 120 Million responsible firearms owners and armed professionals safely possess firearms. Pistols, rifles and shotguns are a constant part of our lives, even if you are not a shooter. Our neighbors, family members, police officers, security guards and firearms industry professionals use firearms for recreation, sport, hunting, defense and various other activities all around us every day without negative impact on anyone.

Unfortunately, these realities are sometimes obscured by tragic events involving guns. These tragedies include heinous crimes, spree killings and accidents. Too often, these events are sensationalized by those who do not understand firearms, firearms owners or our Second Amendment Rights. They are also used to further anti-gun political agendas. The negative outcomes of firearms ownership are tragic. The more educated and responsible we are about firearms, the fewer tragedies there will be.

I have dedicated my adult life to educating those who would own or work with firearms for defensive purposes. I have spent thousands of hours trying to influence and educate the firearms community to be more responsible in the exercise of our rights. I believe strongly that the first and most important step in meeting our responsibilities is education. I have long lamented the lack of firearms safety education in our public school systems. We educate kids about drug abuse, unprotected sex and countless other dangerous things. Firearms can be dangerous, particularly in the hands of uneducated children. Firearms are not inherently evil, nor are they magic talismans against evil. They are inanimate tools, subject to the uses (or misuses) human beings will put them to.

The vast majority of firearms uses in our society are positive. This book is meant to be a starting point for families to discuss this reality. Whether you consider yourself "pro-gun" or "pro-gun control," you have a responsibility as a parent to educate your children honestly about guns. The ubiquity of guns in our country makes education a necessity. It is my hope that this book inspires families to be safer, that it will reduce negative outcomes with firearms and that it might spark new interests in regard to responsible firearms use and ownership in our country.

I have been asked many times over the years how old I think a child should be before they are taught to shoot or educated in gun safety. It is an impossible question for me to answer in absolutes. You, as a parent, must make that decision. I do implore you to take appropriate steps to ensure that your guns are not accessible by children without supervision until they are intellectually and physically capable to use them safely and emotionally mature enough to understand and respect the risks involved. This is the greatest responsibility you have as a gun-owning parent.

-Rob Pincus

My dad has a gun for home protection. He practices with it, and he keeps it locked in a hidden area in his bedroom. He has it in case bad guys try to hurt us in our house.

My mom carries a gun when we are away from the house. She has been to a class and knows how to use it really well, but she only has the gun to protect us.

My grandpa has a gun to go hunting. He likes to spend time in the woods looking for deer.

And when he gets one, he shares the meat with the whole family!

My neighbor has three guns! She shoots almost every weekend and tries to shoot better than her friends.

My cousin has a "BB Gun." It isn't as powerful as a regular gun, but can still hurt people if he doesn't follow the rules. He likes to shoot cans in front of the hill behind his house.

My uncle has a gun because he is a soldier. He fights in faraway places with other soldiers to protect America.

My teacher has a lot of guns. He told us about his collection and how important guns have been in history when people used them to protect themselves and defeat evil leaders.

My mom's Boss has a bodyguard who carries a gun. He is really nice and always wears a fancy suit. My mom says he is trained to protect people.

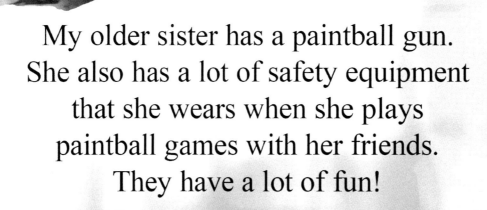

My older sister has a paintball gun.
She also has a lot of safety equipment
that she wears when she plays
paintball games with her friends.
They have a lot of fun!

My aunt has a big gun that she uses to shoot "trap." Trap is a shooting game that lots of people like. One time she shot over 100 targets in a row!

My neighbor has a special gun that he uses to shoot at targets that are very far away. He competes with groups of shooters from all over the world.

My little niece even has her own gun. It is a water pistol that she plays with by the pool. She is not allowed to use it in the house. I think all guns have rules!

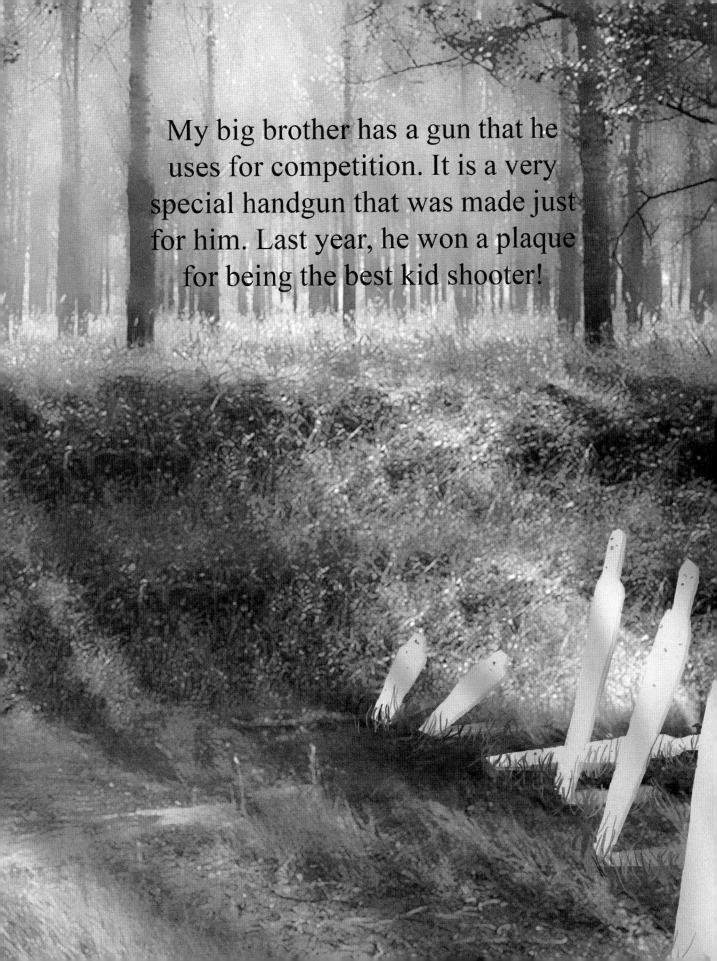

My big brother has a gun that he uses for competition. It is a very special handgun that was made just for him. Last year, he won a plaque for being the best kid shooter!

My grandma has a gun that she likes to shoot with me. It isn't small, but it shoots a very small bullet. It isn't loud or heavy and it is a lot of fun.

My friend's dad works at the bank as a security guard. He has a gun that he wears with his uniform in case bad people try to steal the money or hurt people.

My brother's friend has a special kind of BB Gun called an "airsoft." He can shoot at other people with it during games, as long as they are following the rules and wearing safety masks.

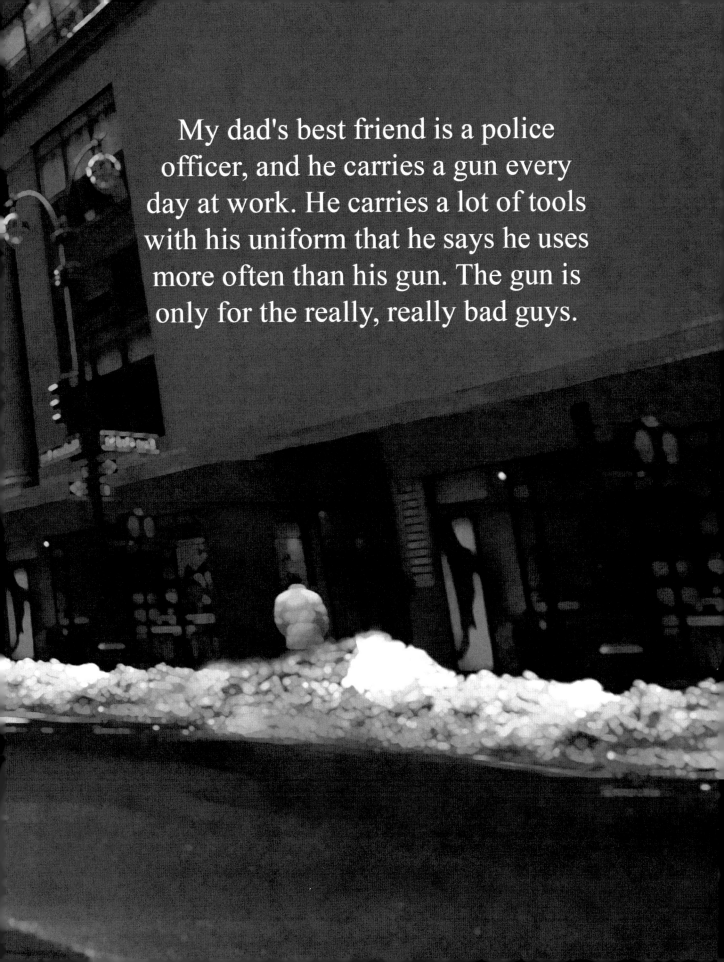

My dad's best friend is a police officer, and he carries a gun every day at work. He carries a lot of tools with his uniform that he says he uses more often than his gun. The gun is only for the really, really bad guys.

The man who lives across the street from us has cowboy guns. He dresses up like a cowboy and goes to the range with his friends. We watched them shoot once, and they were really fast and had a lot of fun.

## About the Author

Rob brings over twenty years of experience in the Gun Industry and a lifetime as a shooter. Rob is one of the gun community's most vocal leaders. He is both an advocate and an educator. His work with United States Concealed Carry Association, National Rifle Association, National Shooting Sports Foundation, Second Amendment Foundation, Personal Defense Network, I.C.E. Training Company and countless other Pro-Gun-Rights Organizations has influenced millions of American Gun Owners to be more responsible and better prepared to defend themselves and those they care about. He has frequently spoken on behalf of responsible gun owners in national and international media. His views are sometimes controversial and often confrontational as he has combated ignorance and negligence around firearms and firearms rights.

Rob is the Executive Vice President of Second Amendment Organization and sits on the boards of The Center for Gun Rights & Responsibilities and Walk The Talk America, an organization addressing issues at the intersection of guns and mental health. Rob has served as a full time or reserve law enforcement officer since 1995 and is the father of two daughters who have been raised around firearms.

Books by Rob Pincus

My Daddy has a Gun, 2020

Defensive Shooting Fundamentals (Level 1 & 2), 2018

Defend Yourself, 2014

Lessons from UNarmed America (with Mark Walters), 2013

Counter Ambush, 2012

Combat Focus Shooting: Evolution 2010, 2010

The Training Log Book, 2008

Combat Focus Shooting, 2006

Made in the USA
Monee, IL
22 April 2021